D0522884

"SUCCESS DOES NOT COME TO THOSE WHO ONLY WORK WHEN THEY FEEL LIKE IT."

- MARK MACIVER

FOREWORD

Culture structures our way of life. It's at the centre of what we do. We see it every day; whether we're walking and talking with people who look and speak like us, or we're interacting with people who might be different to us. Culture influences who we are and, significantly, what we do in life.

That's why focusing on culture is important, this doesn't just mean taking it at face value. It's about challenging our culture, taking back our culture, and redefining what our culture means to us.

It's about what each one of us can do to shape-up our culture so that we can have the greatest impact in our communities.

Mark Maciver is doing just that.

Black culture is not all about entertainment, sports, music, glamour and so on. There are core principles. It's about ethics and hard work, family, solidarity, building community, creating something out of nothing. Mark is all about this. In SliderCuts, he has embodied these principles and created an environment that is a breeding ground for shaping up culture - not just hairlines. The barbershop isn't just a place to come and get a haircut. People from all walks of life and professions visit to hang out, catch up with friends, debate and share personal experiences.

Over the years, Mark has been a backbone to his community, a shining example of progress and hard work. He has taken all his experiences, the good, the bad and the lessons learnt along the way, and created a guide to help those coming up navigate through life and business.

You might see a barber, but what you're really seeing is a businessman, an entrepreneur, a father, a friend, a brother, an uncle, a role model. Mark can relate to the average man. He has been dealt the same cards as many of us, but has made something from nothing. Not everyone needs to be a superstar and you don't always have to be in the limelight to make a difference. It's about what you do with your talents and skills, and how you become the "BEST" at what you do.

"Attract what you expect, reflect what you desire, become what you respect, mirror what you admire."

Keep on building, Mark.

Love and respect,
Dumi Oburota

INTRODUCTION

When I started cutting hair at age 14 I didn't ever think I would be writing this book.

I was just focused on becoming a good barber. The first person I ever cut was myself which went horribly wrong. After that, I quickly became the go-to guy for members of my family, as well as friends and associates in my local area when they couldn't get to the barbershop. Since then, my skills (and my client list) have grown. With over 20 years of experience, I've cut people from babies through to adulthood.

I've worked with well-known people like champion boxer Anthony Joshua, TV presenter Reggie Yates, rappers Tinie Tempah, Stormzy and J. Cole, and NBA basketball player LeBron James, just to name a few: it's been an amazing journey. I've built up a brand that's recognised and respected. I have my own hair and beauty studio. I've been on TV. Done TV adverts, billboards, huge campaigns, won awards, asked to speak publicly and now I'm writing a book!

During my career, I've realised how influential barbers are to communities. Some more than others, but it frustrates me when a barber doesn't use that influence to help shape up their community.

I watched this barbershop show set in America with some celebrities having conversations while getting their haircuts. One of them said that most people in the hood aspire just to make a million dollars. And that hit me because it's the same over here. Growing up, all we ever heard was that if we made a million we had made it and we would be set for life. This could be true, if we knew how to handle the money.

If you were given one hundred thousand pounds, what would you do with it?

I hear people talk about the items they would buy, not thinking about using it to invest into something that could make money on a continual basis. We've been taught how to spend but not how to sustain or make.

I guess I started in business young, then over the years my business acumen grew, and I now find myself giving advice to people. I've never done a business course, so I ask myself: where did this set of skills come from?

When I was seven years old, I was with my three brothers and my mum in our home in Kingsbury, northwest London. We were watching something on TV talking about how much actors were getting paid for films and one of my older brothers Thomas asked: if you got given £40,000 what would you do with it?

Everyone said the things they would buy like trainers, computer consoles, clothes and things like that. I said I would buy a factory to make stuff to sell. My brothers all laughed at me, because they thought it was a silly answer. But I had heard from my mum previously that my granddad used to have a factory making and selling rubber. It was in Benin, Nigeria and he used to even export it to England. This stuck with me and inspired me from a very young age. It made sense to use money to make money, not to just spend it. But moreso, my mum had different businesses at different points when I was growing up that added to my business acumen. She owned a newsagents, did private catering, and also used to make and package chin chin and plantain crisps, Nigerian snacks, that my brothers and I would weigh, package, label and deliver to shops.

One of the most important things in all of this was that my mum included us in all of her business ventures.

My business acumen and curiosity started from a young age, and today I've been able to develop mine through being a barber to create the brand you see now.

I often look for books that are written by people I can relate to, but can never seem to find them. Books by people who are closer to ground level, who talk in a language that is understandable to people like me. Not using terms like: COO, Fiscal Year, Variable Expense, Dividends, Equity, Accounts Receivable. These are all things to learn, but how about a book that talks without the assumption that people know what all these things are?

I was nominated for an Evening Standard Business Award and met a woman who said she was reading a business book and she couldn't understand what these terms meant. This is the same for so many of us.

I started Shaping Up Culture because my culture needed it. I found that a lot of the so-called basic practices weren't being practiced in my community and more than that, weren't known. I have written this basic guide on how to approach business and community.

I've seen so many books from people who are multi-millionaires, talking about how to be one, and I've been told that you have to aim high. I agree, but why don't we read books to be a billionaire or more then? How about we start by getting the approach to business correct?

Most business books cater to a very select sector of society. They assume so much is in place already, like access to financial capital, clear business connections, great networks, good credit - the list goes on.

There don't seem to be any business books that talk about the basics of business. I don't have every answer but I *can* show you the very basics needed before you even have a business plan or an idea. Business ultimately starts with you. The way you see life, the way you conduct yourself, how you respond to things and so on.

This book starts with the foundation, which is you.

THE CONCEPT OF SHAPING UP CULTURE

Shaping Up Culture was birthed in the barbershop. It's a reflection of the conversations happening in the barbershop as well as of the issues that take place in the community and culture I come from: Nigerian heritage, working class, Black Londoner.

The barbershop is a vital part of the Black community.

All the different sects of society have their unofficial community centres: the pub, the member's club, the snooker hall. For a Black man, it's the barbershop. It's a space that allows for discussions and debates to happen. A space where people feel comfortable engaging with other people's different views and opinions. Even more than this, it's where Black men come on a daily basis for help. I always say that as barbers we are unofficial counsellors and therapists – just not all of us are good ones. From giving someone advice on what career path to go down, to offering advice on how to save their marriage, or talking someone through grief, the barbershop is a place of friendship, refuge and advice.

With so many different conversations taking place in the barbershop, and people listening in, it became the perfect place to start shaping up the culture as I had their ears already.

Shaping Up Culture was also born in Dalston, east London: where my wife and I bought our first family home. We were excited to be moving, but we were even more enthusiastic about the move because of the culture that existed in the area. The range of African and Caribbean food shops and other community businesses excited me.

We were so spoiled for choice and when we went to view our flat before we agreed to buy, I discovered that there was a Caribbean food shop just across the road. I remember being excited by that and telling my brother-in-law, Sammy. I felt like I had one up on him, as he used to boast about having a Caribbean restaurant less than 500 metres away from his home.

Fast forward three months: that Caribbean food shop had closed down. I had no idea why. I thought it wasn't a big issue as there were Caribbean and African food shops everywhere. But as we were adjusting to our new surroundings, we started noticing that every few months a Caribbean or African business was closing down.

That's when I heard the term gentrification for the first time. It was everywhere. Gentrification. Gentrification. Gentrification.

For those of you who, like me, didn't know what gentrification meant, the Cambridge Dictionary definition explains: "The process by which a place, especially part of a city, changes from being a poor area to a richer one."

What I witnessed happening was that richer people would come in, buy property cheaply and then the value went up because of their social class. Then they would end up making money from that. This process breaks apart communities who are living within their means but are no longer able to afford living or running businesses in the area, as the demographic and social make-up has changed. Businesses close down and people have to move out of the area because the cost of everything goes up, from business rates and property rent to the price of products in the local shop. Big businesses, such as supermarkets, start taking an interest in the area and smaller businesses like corner shops are no longer able to compete.

Only a certain demographic of businesses were closing down. It didn't make sense, since there were other businesses established by working class people in the area that seemed to be unaffected. I started to think about what those businesses could have done to stay open and why they didn't fight. They just seemed to accept it.

This became a topic of conversation in the barbershop.

As someone with a successful business, who had built up a brand that was generating money and interest, I started talking about what was happening and what I felt people could do. The barbershop became a forum for me to talk about this openly.

You need to support your community, but at the same time you need to be confident that the people you're supporting are providing a good service.

It's not good enough to say you're going to support someone and expect poor services or poor effort. Good quality products and good quality service is vital. I started talking about this continuously. People kept telling me that I delivered messages to them in a way that made it relevant to their lives. Since hearing this and talking in the barbershop, I was inspired to start Shaping Up Culture, a vlog and blog where I talked about different things in the community, business and mentality related, that I felt people in our communities could benefit from.

This is for anyone curious about embarking on a career in business and who needs some knowledge, motivation and direction. It's for those who are at any stage of the journey of life and business. If you are running or planning to run a business, or managing your career at any age, this book is for you. It's a book that I would give to my younger self. Take this as a manual, a basic guide of principles you can apply. My hope is that it will equip you with the knowledge and information as you set off on your journey.

CHAPTER 1

MINDSET

"THE WAY YOU DO SOMETHING, IS THE WAY YOU DO EVERYTHING. YOUR MINDSET SHOULD APPLY TO EVERY ASPECT OF YOUR LIFE AND NOT ONLY WHEN YOU'RE "ON". YOUR ATTITUDE TOWARDS BUSINESS SHOULDN'T DIFFER FROM LIFE."

- REGGIE YATES

The most important thing when setting up and running a business is getting your mind right. It all starts with your mindset.

There are two types of mindsets I come across.

One that encounters obstacles and straight away says: I won't get past this. They then see every reason as to why they can't do it.

The other comes across the same obstacle, but instead says I will get past this, then looks at every option there is to make that happen.

Which mindset do you have?

It's hard for people to succeed in life if they have a negative mindset. This mindset doesn't even allow us to visualise succeeding. If you cannot visualise it, it will be hard to make it happen because it all starts in the mind.

Your body will only do what your mind instructs it to do.

It is important that your mindset is correct, because if you're not up for the fight your actions won't be. Your mentality fights for, or against you. It's you that tells you to get up in the morning and get to work. It's you that decides whether it's a bad or a good day.

The mind is powerful. If you have never thought about the state of your mind, then the time is now. Ask yourself, do I focus more on negative things or positive things? Do I consume more negative media or positive media? What are you consuming? Because that affects the way you think. For example, if you eat junk food it affects your body in look and feel. Your mind is the same, it's affected by the things we take in. What's the ratio between how much you tell yourself 'I can't' vs. 'I can'? Do you mentally discourage or uplift yourself? What are the things you constantly say to yourself?

If you have a more negative mentality, that fights against you, you have to train your mind to start thinking the opposite way. It's not easy and it takes time and consistency. Don't expect everything to change overnight.

I have experienced times when it seemed my body was drained; it couldn't keep going but my mind managed to get more out of a seemingly empty body.

The first time I ran 12 miles, I was at mile 10 when my body felt like no more could be done. I was at a point of nearly crying, but my mind told me 'don't stop, keep going' and I finished the run.

My mindset was the same when I rode my bicycle to Brighton from Holloway, on the hottest day of the year in a jumper (I hadn't realised how hot it was). And it was the same when I was in college and I stayed up all night finishing an essay even though my body was fighting to sleep. You might not realise it, but you can do a lot more than you think.

People who go the furthest in life are the people who dream the biggest and believe those dreams will become reality. I don't want it to sound like I'm saying 'if you have the right mindset you will achieve whatever you want'. But, if you shift the way you think, the chances of you succeeding are a lot higher and will bring you closer, even in failure, to your goals. The right mindset will help you when dealing with setbacks and failures.

When you adopt a 'can-do' mindset, you may not know how things will happen, but you become open to finding ways that they will.

I'm sharing this from my experience of building SliderCuts.

Setting up and running a business is exhausting work, both physically and mentally, so it's important you get your mind right. The journey of life can be hard and even harder if your mind isn't fighting for you.

So work on your mindset and make sure it's working for, and not against, you.

CHAPTER 2
GOALS

"KNOW WHAT YOUR GOAL IS, DON'T GUESS IT... IF YOU DON'T KNOW WHAT YOUR GOALS ARE YOU'RE NEVER GOING TO REACH THEM."

– IDRIS ELBA

When it comes to goals, people always put money at the top of the list. Let's clear this up before I get into it: you should never be chasing money.

Money is just a mediator between you and your goals. The goal should be the thing you want i.e. buying that house, those new pair of trainers, learning to play an instrument or whatever it is you want. Money will then be a mediator between you and that goal you're pursuing, a means to help you reach it.

Saying your goal is to get money is like a builder who wants to build a house saying their goal is to get bricks and cement. The bricks and cement are just part of the process.

Money in itself means nothing if it's not followed by a transaction. What you want to do with the money has the substance.

Start thinking about what your actual goals are. Do you want to spend more time with your friends? Do you want to lose weight? Do you want to enter the World Guinness Book of Records by owning the world's largest collection of toothbrushes? Whatever that goal is, the point is for you to start correctly setting them.

The first step is to think about what it is you actually want out of life - what it is you want to do and achieve - write it down. Don't think or worry about what other people want, just work out what YOU want to do and then you can start the journey towards it.

Everybody has something that they want and your first goal should be to figure that out. Once you have that, make sure you know your reason to the goals this will help you stay motivated.

You may ask 'what about those people who don't know what their goals are, what do they do if they don't know what they want out of life?'

Everybody wants something out of life; even if you don't think you do or don't know what you want. Often people are focused on what other people are doing or what other people want them to do. This can cause distractions to what you want out of life.

Go back to basics. Ask yourself, what do I like? What do I enjoy? What is important to me and what changes would I like to see in myself and the world?

Answer these questions and you will find some of your goals. This may take some time to work out and your answers at different points in life can change and that's okay. Your answers will make it easier to choose a career path. One that either assists or encompasses your goals.

When it comes to pursuing goals, there are four elements needed for success: time, effort, currency and consistency.

Time and effort go hand in hand. Any successful thing needs time and effort put into it. These two things work best together. There's no point putting in 10 hours a day doing nothing. You also need to put in currency. I say currency and not money.

Money is definitely a massive help and would make things a lot easier, but if you don't have it, there are other ways. You can use trade and exchange your talents and skills with other people. As a barber I could offer someone five free haircuts in exchange for them designing a flyer for me. Both things hold value. Don't rule yourself out just because you don't have money. If you need money and you have none, there are loans, investment, selling shares, selling things you have, etc - explore all the options.

You have to consistently put in time, effort and currency. The main elements that are needed for a plant to grow and live a healthy life are consistent sunlight, air, water and good soil.

If you gave a plant all of the things it needed for a month and then stopped for five months and then gave it for two months then stopped for another seven months the plant would die because you gave it the right elements but lacked consistency.

Knowing your reasons is your fuel.

"Go home and write down the reason why you're running…"
Charlie Dark, Run Dem Crew

A few years ago, I joined Run Dem Crew and ran a half marathon. Run Dem Crew is a running club built on community focusing on creating connections and building relationships, as well as running!

When I joined, I spoke with the owner, Charlie Dark, and explained my goals. I wanted to complete the half marathon and I wanted to do it in under two hours.

He said: "Great, we can help you do that, but I need you to go home and write down the reason why you're running."

The next week I went back with my reason and he told me he didn't want to see it, the reason was for me, not him.

"Everyone is running for a reason. You need to know the reason why you're running because when things get hard and you hit the wall, which you will do, knowing the reason as to why you're running will be the thing that keeps you going."

He was correct. There were many times when I hit the wall when I was training for this challenge, and the main thing that kept me going was remembering my reason for running.

Your goal is the destination you're trying to get to, you are the vehicle, and your reason is the fuel that will keep driving you forwards.

It's important to know that the journey to your goals isn't always easy. Setting goals correctly is the start, but you also need to understand that the journey to your goals is actually where all the work goes in. Everybody's journey is a different length. The journey may not be smooth but when you look at anybody's success story, the journey is where all the work happened.

CHAPTER 3
MAKE YOURSELF VALUABLE

"WHATEVER YOU DO, WORK AT IT WITH ALL YOUR HEART, AS WORKING FOR GOD, NOT FOR HUMAN BOSSES."

COLOSSIANS 3:23

I encounter people who are in uncertain situations - people living in fear of being cut. My advice is always: make yourself valuable. But the question is, how?

There are three types of people I generally come across:

1. Those who don't do what they're supposed to do and have excuses as to why.

2. Those that do what their job requires, nothing more and nothing less.

3. Those that go above and beyond, doing what they're supposed to do and more.

Which type of person are you?

You can fluctuate between all three of these types in life, but the third person generally always receives opportunities and is regularly recommended.

I had a conversation with someone who was in a job that they felt unstable in. They weren't sure if their boss was going to keep them on so in response they further slacked off.

Through their fear of losing their job, they chose not to work properly their attitude was 'I might be losing my job anyway', and they were fired anyway.

Their attitude and work ethic let them down. This person said to me they weren't sure if they were going to be kept on anyway, which seemed like they were justifying their slackness. Just like the first person described, they found an excuse as to why they were not doing what they should be.

By making yourself valuable, especially when it comes to business, you make yourself an asset. If your company needs to make cuts due to budget, you want to put yourself in a position where you're the last one they want to let go of because of your value.

Make yourself an asset, not a liability.

An asset: a useful or valuable thing or person.

A liability: a person or thing whose presence or behaviour is likely to put one at a disadvantage.

In my career, the thing that has helped get the best out of me and make me an asset, is a verse I read in the Bible in Colossians 3:23:

"Whatever you do, work at it with all your heart, as working for God, not for human bosses."

My boss is God, and He is always watching. Imagine if your boss was always around you when you were working. They would always get the best out of you because you would work to a certain level.

I was always getting checked when I was slacking, cutting corners or not doing work to the level I should be. This got the best out of me and helped me to get to where I am today.

Often, we try and do just enough to tick the boxes but those who are assets and valuable operate like the third person – ticking all the boxes and doing more. Life can be cutthroat; people generally want the best person for a job or the person who's willing to give most to that job. Now don't get yourself taken advantage of, but understand with value comes power. People won't know your value if you don't show them. Make yourself valuable. People want to hold onto things of value.

CHAPTER 4
THE STRUGGLE
IS REAL

You need to understand, in order to expand and grow you need to stretch and stretching is painful but beneficial.

Everybody talks about their story.

It's a beautiful thing that inspires, teaches and warns others. However a lot of people don't talk about the struggle while they are in it. This chapter was originally a vlog that I had done and released while I was in the midst of the struggle.

It was important to talk about the struggle while I was going through it to show the reality and the journey, patience, faith and perseverance in real time.

One of the defining moments of SliderCuts was opening my shop in October 2018. That year I won three awards. I was one of the faces of a Facebook nationwide campaign which saw me in a TV advert and on billboards all around the UK. My face was all over taxis and on the Underground with iZettle. I was in a partnership with Reebok and a Nike advert called "Nothing Beats a Londoner".

From the outside everything looked amazing, but the work, effort and struggle that went in is important.

The struggle is real.

In 2015, I decided to open up my own shop. Location was the most important thing. I wanted it to be in Shoreditch. There was a big Afro-Caribbean population (which is the area I specialise in), but there were no Afro hair barber shops or hairdressers. A gap in the market. I wanted to find somewhere that had parking and I needed the shop to be near a train station, and to have buses that stopped nearby. The space and size had to be right too.

It took me a year and a half to find the right

location. I started looking for places online. When this failed, I decided to go knocking on the doors of businesses in locations I liked asking if they'd be willing to sell. One said yes. I ended up waiting 12 to 18 months for the lease to become available, but it was worth it. The whole process took three years.

Mentally that was hard, knowing I had a space I wanted but couldn't get access to. During this three-year period I bought a three bedroom flat for my family. A struggle in itself because I had to put down a 25% deposit to get it on a buy to-let, then wait two years before I could move in.

A year after the barbershop space finally became available I had no money. I had to figure out a way to make SliderCuts happen.

I needed to find between £150,000 to £200,000 and I had to find it fast. I knew I didn't want any investors. I had spent so much of my own time, energy and money building up a recognisable and respected brand. I had a vision of how I wanted SliderCuts to be and thought others being involved would compromise that. Plus I knew the value of SliderCuts would go up once the shop opened.

This decision made the process very difficult because at that time I had NOTHING. Some would say this was a stupid decision but I knew I had good 'SOCIAL CREDIT' (check out the social credit chapter to find out what this is).

I encountered bad builders who didn't finish the work but I paid them in full before it was finished. I felt like everything was going wrong. Many days I'd wake up in the morning with more and more obstacles in my way, all while being a working dad and husband. This is where your mindset fights for or against you.

I took out some very high interest loans from loan companies and friends, maxed out every credit card and took literally every penny out of my accounts.

When I finally found all the money I thought I needed, I was still tens of thousands of pounds short as I never budgeted for going over budget.

The pressure was real.

My faith became my most important asset, because I heard a word from God:

"Pay whatever needs to be paid on that day and then sort out the next day when it comes."

A simple concept but applying it was difficult. There were times when my mortgage had to be paid the next day but a water bill was due on the present day. But I told myself to stick to the words I heard from God and my faith showed out because it came to pass.

I paid between £70,000 to £100,000 in interest on loans. Taking out these loans instead of investments caused stress and put pressure on me and my family. The lack of spare time because I was working all hours of the day, no holidays, no mind space, having less and less energy. Money was spent before it came in. The debt, strain and stress snowballed but what kept me going was my faith, remembering what my goal was and my reason.

In order to expand and grow you need to stretch. Stretching is painful but beneficial.

Patience was required on this journey and I finally opened up the shop while building works were still going on. I opened up SliderCuts in a world of debt and unfinished building works. Two months in, I had three senior barbers and a hairdressers' space at the back of the shop that was empty. I took on two apprentices and paid them out of my own pocket. You have to invest in both your future and the future of others.

Eight months after opening, the shop was paying for itself, one of the apprentices I took on became a junior barber and I had three hairdressers working part-time. Things finally started lining up with the vision.

It's important that I am open with my journey to show others there is no shame in sharing your struggle. A lot of the time people think they are the only ones struggling, or they look at other people and think they had it easier. It's important you are aware of the realities that come with starting and running a business. It's not fair to paint the picture as perfect but instead, be honest with people.

The struggle isn't embarrassing, the struggle is part of the process that produces the results. This is what you see when the shutters go up at SliderCuts, the results of faith, hard work, patience and perseverance.

The struggle is real, and whenever you're building something special, it's never easy.

CHAPTER 5

THE MISCONCEPTION OF BEING ORGANIC

Don't allow your misconceptions to stunt your growth. Growing something without the use of chemicals or unnatural resources is creating organic produce.

The misconception is that pushing your product out or paying for promotions is unnatural, when it is a natural process of growing and expanding. This misunderstanding has caused many businesses to fail.

I've come across many people who have this mindset. They almost feel guilty pushing themselves or their business. People think that if they pay to promote their business, they are "buying" their success, when you are actually investing into it.

Facebook, Google, Amazon, Netflix, Coca Cola and Apple are examples of extremely successful businesses that have invested hundreds of millions into marketing, promotions and strategy.

They didn't just create a product and leave it for people to discover themselves hoping that word of mouth would get around.

How can you expect people to find out about, and buy into your business if they can't see it or don't know about it? How can you expect to improve the sales of your product if people don't know where to buy it? Good promotion is often promotion you have to pay for.

I've felt awkwardness and guilt at times when I've paid to promote SliderCuts in different ways and this used to make me feel inorganic.

As a community, we are behind, and my fear is that we'll be stuck in this position if we don't switch up our thought process.

Here's a hypothetical example of this: two people released a song and they both uploaded it to all the main digital platforms. One singer had the idea to let it grow naturally, or 'organically' and not use any of the relevant social media cues, hashtags or even schedule its release. The second musician thought differently. They released their song on the same day but instead of just seeing what happened, they pushed the song. They sent messages to their friends on WhatsApp, they put the link in their social media bio, they posted the song on their social media platforms every three to six posts, and they paid for promotions so people that didn't follow them also see their song as well as their platform.

After one month, the results showed out. The first person got 300 streams, the second got 10,000 streams. The first person looked down on the second because they felt they had taken an inorganic route. The second felt they did what was organic in business.

Whose process was really organic?

This attitude is something I've seen so often and it's a mindset that needs to change.

It is a natural process of business to promote, strategise and invest. Ask yourself, what are my actual goals? Is it to put stuff out there and just see what happens? Or is it to build a successful business that will help your life?

Don't allow your misconceptions to stunt your growth.

CHAPTER 6
OUT OF
SIGHT
OUT OF
MIND

"MY PAINTINGS
CARRY MESSAGES.
I LOVE TO WORK ON
MASSIVE PUBLIC
WALLS, BECAUSE
THEY REACH AND
ARE SEEN BY SO
MANY PEOPLE."

- LAKWENA
  MACIVER

Networking is important to remain connected to people, but it's even more important that you stay in people's sight and on their mind.

We need to stay on people's radars if we want to be remembered when opportunities arise. Everyone's been in a situation where they've either been forgotten, or forgotten someone. Usually, this is because, they've been completely out of sight.

Let's say you're throwing a party and you forget to invite a friend. It could look like you didn't want them there, when really they just weren't on your mind.

It's the same thing with business. For example, in a situation where we've been looking for a plumber or an electrician we end up searching for someone who's sitting right under our noses.

If you're offering a service of any sort, you have to stay at the forefront of people's minds.

This means regularly reminding people of what you do. People will not just remember because you are good at what you do or because you've told them once. We are all constantly flooded with adverts from different people selling what they do.

Our brains can't store all the information we get bombarded with every day. Look at the amount of brands that promote through clothing, billboards, buses and more. I walk around wearing SliderCuts merchandise so when people see me, they see the brand; this is me advertising to you.

Go on to any one of your social media platforms and straight away someone will be selling something to you. You might not know it, but they are.

As a barber every time I post a picture or video of a haircut, I'm selling my services to you. The more regularly I put stuff out, the more likely it is that I'll stay in your head.

Make sure your brand is seen in the right spaces. Where your target audience is, that's where you should be. One of the main places to be 'seen' by large amounts of people is social media. Facebook, Instagram, YouTube, Snapchat, Twitter. These platforms have so much reach that, whatever service you provide; there will be an audience there for you. But to just be on these platforms is not enough. You have to be consistent with your content.

It's not enough for me to post once saying, "Hey, I'm a barber, come and get a haircut." If applicable, put your actual work on these platforms. If you're a barber, post your haircuts. If you're a personal trainer, post workouts. If you're an artist, post your artwork. People won't just remember you out of the blue if you don't regularly show them what you do.

It's not always the best person that gets chosen for a job. A lot of the time it's the best person that came to mind. To reach success, make sure you keep in sight to stay in mind.

People won't just remember you out of the blue if you don't show them what you do. The world is always moving, and the people in it are moving too, so you've got to stay in people's minds.

CHAPTER 7

TEAM WORK

"BUILDING THE RIGHT TEAM TO SUPPORT YOUR VISION IS ONE OF THE MOST IMPORTANT ASPECTS OF BUSINESS AND LIFE SUCCESS. SURROUND YOURSELF WITH EXPERTS IN THE SKILLS YOU NEED AND DON'T HAVE, ENSURING YOU GIVE THEM CLEAR DIRECTION AND OBJECTIVES TO ACHIEVE."

- TIM CAMPBELL

"Many hands make light work." The importance of having help is everyone needs to have different tasks and positions to achieve the goal effectively.

In my experience of running a business and seeing others who have successful businesses, the common trait we all share is a well-run team around us.

I have the brand that I have because I've had good ideas but more importantly, I know how to call on people who know or do things better than me.

I put my success down to the team I've had, officially and unofficially. My wife, my brother, my executive assistant, my publicist, my team coordinator - the list goes on! Everything is a team sport.

The basics of building a team is the understanding that everyone has a part to play.

There is no point finding ten people who are amazing at the exact same thing. In a game of football there would be no point having eleven amazing strikers on the pitch, regardless of how good they are individually, they are only good for the position and role they play. A good team is filled with people playing their positions, from answering calls, responding to emails, strategists, marketers, HR, publicists, sales and so on.

To find a good team you first have to be honest about your strengths, weaknesses and the position you yourself play within your vision.

Honesty about yourself is a massive strength in business; it will allow you to make informed decisions.

Looking at my own strengths and weaknesses, and finding people that fill my weak areas, has helped me in the long run. Know your limitations.

You have to take time to find the right team and make sure you ask all the right questions.

When I hired my PA, it was a five-step process.

A CV and a brief description as to why she wanted the job. An email interview with a few questions being asked back and forth. A phone call with my publicist - as she was qualified to oversee the recruitment process. A brief assessment task. An in-person interview with myself.

Make sure you spend time picking and finding the right team members, which might involve hiring and firing till you get it right, which is fine. You won't always get it right straight away, but the process will all be worth it when you eventually find the right team.

CHAPTER 8

THE SO-CALLED OVERNIGHT SUCCESS

"MY OVERNIGHT SUCCESS WAS 10 YEARS IN THE MAKING."

- SHARMADEAN REID

There's no such thing as an overnight success.

Most of the time people call someone an overnight success, because they haven't taken time to consider or look into the process that got that person to where they are. That doesn't mean they weren't working before you discovered them, they just weren't on your radar.

Take Michael Dapaah, aka Big Shaq. For those who believe he was an overnight success, have you examined his process and how long he was working on what he was doing before he blew up with 'Man's Not Hot?'

He put time into creating shows, even having a failed show that a lot of people don't know about. He didn't let that stop him. Instead he came back and created a new show called 'SWIL ('Somewhere In London') which was a success and took off way before his BBC Radio 1Xtra appearance blew up. He had sketches that were getting likes and views on Instagram, and a following of about 250,000. People think he just ended up on Charlie Sloth's Fire in the Booth, but he planned it. He had put it on his vision board and he made it happen.

These are the things people ignore when they label someone an overnight success. They ignore the hard work, the failures, the energy and effort that has gone into getting to the place where you know who they are.

This is why it's important for us to know about the process. If you ever see a success story and you're looking to go down that same road, study that person's process, not the result. Those who only focus on the results don't appreciate how much goes into the outcome.

Look at Anthony Joshua. He trains intensely for hours a day, five days a week, for four months straight just for a 30-minute fight. More work goes into the process than the actual fight on the day. This applies to all fields. Musicians spend more time rehearsing than actually performing.

I did a campaign with Instagram where they got 12-16 hours' worth of footage over a two-day shoot, to create a 15 second clip.

More work goes into the process than it seems when the finished product is presented to us. With the Facebook campaign, I was shooting for eight hours taking hundreds of pictures just to get that one picture that made it to the billboard. From shooting different angles, to changing positions, moving the set up around and more, so much went into getting that one picture.

Don't believe in the myth of the overnight successes, if you look closely at any of these stories, you're likely to find years' worth of work behind it.

This is the reality you don't often see: the hard work during the process. If you're not ready for that hard work, maybe you're not ready for success.

CHAPTER 9

YOU'RE ALWAYS IN AN INTERVIEW

"THE PERSON YOU ARE WHEN NO ONE IS LOOKING, IS THE PERSON YOU SHOULD BE WORKING ON. IT'S THIS PERSON'S CHARACTER THAT SLIPS OUT AT THE WRONG TIMES."

- MARK MACIVER

You are always in an interview, whether you realise it or not.

Quite often, the person we are when we're in a private setting with our friends or family, is different to the person we are when we're in public. Our connections with our friends and family is going to be much stronger than with strangers or acquaintances. However, the person you want to be when the right person is around, should be the person you want to become.

The right person comes in different shapes, shades and costumes. You never know when the right person will be watching you.

The right person is the person who is in a position to help you. That could be someone hiring for the job you want, the investor you've been looking for, someone who could vouch for you.

This is how I came to cut J. Cole's hair. I was doing a favour for my sister-in-law, who had asked me to cut a friend's hair. Her friend, Eddie, came to the shop and sat in my chair. I treated him as I would any of my customers: with respect, politeness and great customer service. He left happy and with a clean shape-up. Fast-forward a couple of months, and I'm in Church on a Sunday. I see a couple of missed calls from Eddie, so step out to call him back, and it turns out he's with J Cole, who's in need of a haircut but couldn't reach his barber.

You can't determine which situations or interactions will develop into opportunities and, in the same vein, you shouldn't treat each situation or interaction with the mindset that you're getting something out of it. It's disingenuous, people will see straight through that. But you never want to leave a situation and think, 'did I miss that opportunity because I didn't act right?'

If you think no one is watching and you've got Facebook, Instagram, Twitter or Snapchat, then think again. If you're putting 'stuff' out there, that 'stuff' is being watched. You are always in an interview and you, too, are always interviewing other people. Whether it's a customer in your chair, the person sitting in your shop, life is an interview.

Treat people with respect, since you never know who you are going to meet again.

You're always in an interview – be ready – you could be presented with an opportunity you've wanted your whole life.

CHAPTER 10
SOCIAL CREDIT

"BEING FAMOUS DOESN'T MEAN YOU'RE LIVING WELL OR YOUR FAMILY ARE LOOKED AFTER, IT MEANS YOU'RE FAMOUS, YOU ARE WELL-KNOWN. DOING GREAT BUSINESS WITH PEOPLE YOU TRUST IS WHAT CAN SECURE YOUR FAMILY'S RESOURCES."

- ANTHONY JOSHUA

Social credit: the value you hold among your peers, friends and others.

Social credit works similarly to the official credit scoring system, except your credit is built on your interactions with people.

Social credit comes down to you keeping your word and standing by what you've said, as well as taking responsibility when you have vouched for someone.

It's the first credit score you'll ever have in life and starts being built from when you're young. This is when people will start to build a picture of how they view you and whether you're deemed trustworthy or not.

Will you pay back the 50p someone lent you?

Will you give back the football you borrowed from your friend?

Will you be on time to meet someone, or will you be late or not show up at all?

All these things play into the picture people start creating of you. This can impact how they deal with or talk about you and can even impact any business they go on to do with you later in life.

A lot of the time people's opinions of others come from their dealings with them or what they have seen or heard about them.

The harsh reality of life is that it's the bad things that stick in people's minds the longest. You could do ten amazing things but the one bad thing people will remember you for. With work you can build up your social credit by putting out good seeds instead of bad ones with all your dealings. The bad seeds tend to grow ten times faster than the good ones.

When I first opened my shop, I had maxed out on my official credit. I couldn't get any more loans, but I still had a lot of debt to pay. This is where my good social credit came in. About thirteen different people helped me out, from lending me money or being a guarantor on loans, to one person paying for his next two years' worth of haircuts upfront to help me. The only reason they did these things for me, is because they trusted I would fulfill what I said I would.

Have integrity, and honour your word. Make sure you are someone people can trust and rely upon. It's for your personal benefit that you keep your name good.

CHAPTER 11

SHAPING UP YOUR COMMUNITY

"IF I DO IT OUT OF LOVE IT'S NOT TO BENEFIT MYSELF."

- STORMZY

In order for a community to flourish, those in the community that are more privileged have to teach those who are not. If you learn a skill, that talent you have should be taught to others that may not be as advantaged as you. Within the class and community I've come from, there isn't a lot of money or things to do. In these settings, no money and boredom often leads to the wrong things and this is why it's so important for everybody to play their part.

Nobody makes it without help, there is no such thing as 'self-made'. I would be a liar and ungrateful if I said I did it all myself. I definitely put in the hard work and went out there looking for opportunities. I'm God made, family and community raised. The amount of people in my family and community that have added to my life can't go unnoticed.

Since I've been helped, I need to do the same.

Love is what is needed, and love is sacrifice.

As Stormzy said: "If I do it out of love it's not to benefit myself."

It doesn't necessarily have to be money; it could be your time, connections, facilities, words, spending money in the community or all of them and more. Whatever you choose, know that you are contributing to the growth and advancement of the community.

We can make a community more self-sufficient by helping to teach trades and skills to those coming up.

This is what Shaping Up Culture is all about.

If I need a plumber or electrician, for example, I'll always look locally first.

Shaping Up Culture is about equipping people with the skills they need to do things correctly so that people can call on them.

When it comes to bettering the community, we need to do more than talk. Most of us know what to say and have the answers, but few actively do the things that are needed. Many will say it's not fair that when someone gets a criminal record, they can't get a job, but how many of us are willing to hire those people? It's up to business owners, community leaders and people who understand the issues to be the ones that affect change.

I try my best to put my money where my mouth is.

I'm open to the people I hire and prefer to give people chances instead of judging them based on their past. People judge previous criminal offenders or those with a chequered past. But why do that when you can be the change they need to turn their lives around? That's when communities thrive.

The selfish mindset only thinks about what is best for them, but the community mindset thinks about what is best for all.

I hire young people to come in and I pay to train them up. My shop is already full of barbers which means I'm essentially training up people I know I can't hire so they can go and work somewhere else.

But, if I'm looking out for my community, then that's a sacrifice that has to be made.

This is how we create a good community, continuously planting these morals of 'I help you; you help someone else'.

You don't have to give money if you can't afford to.

Give your time, efforts, anything. Give something.

I was cutting hair for Virgil Abloh from Louis Vuitton at Paris Fashion Week, and in a brief conversation, I said to him, "Thanks for pushing the culture forward."

"We are doing it together", he responded.

You see, community and culture doesn't sit on one person's shoulders, it's something that everyone has to put into.

The key to building a good community is everybody putting in and the affirmation from those more socially influential to acknowledge the pennies that make up the pounds. If individuals understood that there is strength in numbers, people would understand how valuable they are in the community.

Before pointing the finger at others, look in the mirror and ask yourself 'what am I doing to effect change?' We all have a part to play.

Shaping up your community is a team effort. If it takes a village to raise a child, then how much more for a community?

FINAL THOUGHTS

When I started Shaping Up Culture, I didn't realise I was writing a book. I was just putting out vlogs and blogs and sharing pieces of advice that I thought the community and culture needed to hear.

These vlogs and blogs were received well, and I had people commenting, messaging and coming up to me to say how helpful it was for them.

This book originally never even had a theme but the more I wrote the more it became apparent that it was about business, community and culture as I couldn't get away from writing on topics that touch on them. This book is a guide on how to approach them.

Like I said in the intro, so often those who know make the assumption that the very basics and foundations are known. This is a problem because people end up teaching the ladder of success without the first five steps. Which makes sense as to why people wouldn't be advancing, because you think you're on the ladder but you're actually just looking up at it.

I hope you take these valuable lessons from my journey in life and in business.

We've all heard, a wise person learns from their mistakes, but I think the wiser person learns from the mistakes and examples of others. You don't need to go wrong to then go right. You can start the journey on the right path.

Communities find it hard to get ahead when every generation has to start again.The aim should be to put our children in a starting position that is further ahead from where we started. This happens through knowledge, connections and businesses.

I can't pass all these things to everyone, but the thing I can pass to you all is knowledge.

ACKNOWLEDGMENTS

There are many ways in which people have helped me in writing this book. Whether by listening, doing dictation, giving me advice on the structure, or playing a part in my journey that led me to be able to offer this information I'm giving, thank you.

Firstly, I would like to thank God for allowing me to be a tool to help and inspire others. My heart for these issues came from Him. I can't take credit for the morals and principles written in this book; these are the biblical principles I've learnt and tried to live by. Jesus (Yahushua) is the example I'm trying to mirror. So the good you see in me is a reflection of Him.

Lakwena Maciver - You are always involved in some way or another in all my dealings. Whether designing something, correcting my grammar, listening to me or looking after our children when I'm having to work. You were there from the beginning of this project, even helping to come up with the name SHAPING UP CULTURE. You weren't even hired on this project but you still ended up designing my front cover! Thank you.

Casey Elisha - To date, the best Executive Assistant I have had. Thank you for all the dictation you took continuously in a noisy barbershop, for challenging some of the points in this book and helping to keep my English A* worthy !

Shaffra Gray-Read - Thank you for transcribing some of my Shaping Up Culture vlogs to blogs and helping to turn my spoken thoughts into words to be read. Also can't forget you were part of the brainstorming team that came up with the name SHAPING UP CULTURE.

Marcia Norbal - Thank you for transcribing some of my vlog into written pieces. These helped me to see my thoughts through my eyes as written words.

Alex Reads - Thank you for editing the book and going through the back and forths along the way.

Mide Ola-Said - Thank you for reading over my book before I handed it in and advising me on how to make my points stronger, and making me understand the difference between speaking and writing.

Thank you to **Aimée Felone, David Stevens, Marssaié Jordan** and the whole Knights Of team. Marssaié, for connecting me with Knights Of as well as designing and structuring the book, and Aimée and David for believing in and signing on to the project. You guys have been supportive and available on the phone whenever I called to hear me out and I'm thankful for that.

Doreen Uwaifo - Thank you to my mother. You taught me great work ethic through actions, always working and doing your best to provide for me and my brothers. All the businesses you ran subconsciously taught me and having us involved to see it all up front provided great lessons that will always stick with me.

Thomas Maciver - What an example of hard working. Growing up watching you wake up every day at about 4am to go to work added to my work ethic. You were doing these early morning starts way before me and Peter.

Philip Maciver - Who is no longer with us. He taught me to just do and not make excuses, to find a way to make things happen. His life and death showed me that tomorrow might not come so do the things you want to do today and I'm thankful he lived that way.

Peter Maciver - Thank you because you are one of my biggest supporters and that is in action. The amount of money you have lent me to help support my business ventures. Also our friendly competition between each other helps to keep us on our toes!

Dumi Oburota - Thank you for the kind words you wrote in the foreword of this book, for always being someone I can talk to about business when I need advice and for just being a good business example.

Last but not least, thank you to each individual who provided a quote that was added to the book. All the quotes included in Shaping Up Culture were personally given to me, so thank you to:

Anthony Joshua

Idris Elba

Lakwena Maciver

Reggie Yates

Sharmadean Reid

Stormzy

Tim Campbell